This book is dedicated
to my mother,
Barbara H. Fukumoto

Mahalo Nui

I would like to acknowledge and sincerely thank Debbie Chaiprakorb from *Creations by You* for the concept of creating a money folds origami book. Mahalo also to Sharon Weathers for the *Slipper* idea, to Linda Ige for suggesting the *'Ukulele*, and to my daughter, Kiara, for proposing the *Shell* (even though it was not the shell she had in mind), to my neighbors, Rose Oda, Hideko Uesugi, and Julie Young for the foliage used in backgrounds and leis. A very special mahalo to my niece Quinn Fukumoto for "being there" and to Lewis Harrington, for the beautiful photography. I would also like to express my gratitude (once again) to *Island Heritage*.

THE GUIDE TO
Island—Style
MONEY FOLDS

by
Jodi Fukumoto

ISLAND HERITAGE™
PUBLISHING

TABLE OF CONTENTS

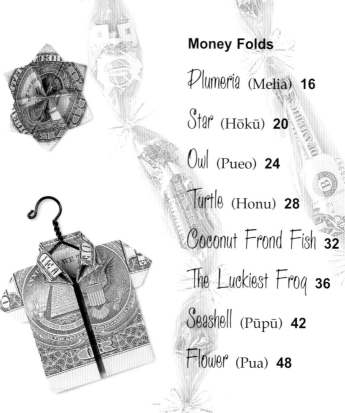

Foreword

Practiced since the Edo era (1603-1867) in Japan, the art of origami traces its origin to the Chinese art of paper folding. The art was brought to Japan in the sixth century by Buddhist monks who introduced paper to Japan. Japanese history documents that samurai warriors exchanged gifts adorned with *noshi*, a good luck token made of folded strips of paper. Origami butterflies were also used during the celebration of *shinto* (a Japanese religion) weddings to represent the bride and groom. Perhaps these were some of the earliest uses of origami.

The term "origami" is derived from two Japanese words—*oru* meaning "to fold," and *kami* meaning "paper." It is the Japanese art of paper folding to create a representation of an object using geometric folds and crease patterns preferably without the use of gluing or cutting the paper medium.

Although origami traces its origins to Japan, money folding is not a Japanese craft. Using origami as a basis, money folding is another way of creating numerous shapes to express ones creativity, adding crafted value to any monetary denomination.

Today, folded money is used for numerous expressions of good luck and best wishes for all occasions including birthdays, graduations, funerals, and holidays. Many are also used as amulets or as mementos. A pineapple for housewarmings, owls for graduations, frogs for luck during Vegas ventures are just some of the uses of symbolic money folds. Slippers are also popular island-style symbols of a good luck wish as one embarks on a journey. Money folds are also used as favors, centerpieces, party tokens and are sewn into lei, the perfect way to present these creations in a popular island-style tradition.

First published in 2002, and originally titled *Hawaiian-Style Money Folds*, *Island-Style Money Folds* has become a top-selling craft book in Hawai‘i and beyond. With over 150,000 copies sold, the universal appeal of folding money into shapes with island flair makes this how-to book the perfect gift or souvenir for crafters of any age. Illustrated, step-by-step guides to transforming any monetary denomination into delightful gifts or décor make seemingly unimaginable shapes possible to create.

Additional money fold ideas can be found in the *The Guide to American Money Folds* and *Funny Money Folds for Kids* also published by Island Heritage. Visit www.welcometotheislands.com for more folding fun.

(Note: This guide introduces color-coding to its model instructions to help the beginner understand the art of origami by clarifying and defining every fold, so be sure to read Color-Coded Instructions before beginning.)

Supplies

In addition to cash, have on hand origami paper in 6-inch square and larger sizes for envelopes and boxes, paper clips, high-quality toothpicks, and double-stick tape. Check the individual model instructions for any other specific needs.

To use paper instead of money, you will need a ruler, pencil, and scissors to measure and cut paper to proper dimensions. (See *Paper Substitutions*.)

❖   ❖   ❖

Presenting Money

The Right Bill
Before selecting a bill for a particular model, study the folded example and read the information at the beginning of the instructions, which offers suggestions on bills to use. In general, the back of the one dollar bill is favored—it is a practical choice that provides good color and design to most models.

As you may know, bills of higher denominations bear either an old or a current design. Bills with the old design usually work as well as the one dollar bill in terms of color and design; however, they are slowly being pulled from circulation and can be hard to find, especially in good condition. Those with the current design are somewhat plain and often produce less interesting models lacking in color; models created from these bills are included as examples mainly because of the bills' availability.

Gift Idea
Rather than fold a large denomination bill that must be unfolded to be spent, add a model to your gift that is folded from a one dollar bill that can be saved as a keepsake.

Model Care

To ensure that your gift doesn't unfold:

1. Use a new, clean, crisp bill. It not only makes a nicer model and gift, it is easier to crease and will hold a fold better than a used bill.
2. Iron the bill on medium heat to remove any moisture. If you are using a less-than-new bill, ironing can also remove creases.
3. After, or even during, folding, iron your model to set folds.
4. Use double-stick tape between layers that tend to separate. Do not use glue.
5. If you fold your gift in advance of giving it, use paper clips to hold it and continue to "set" folds until you are ready to present it.
6. Store models in an air-tight container or plastic bag.
7. Store two-dimensional models between the pages of a heavy book.

Leis or Garlands

To "string" most money models into leis, use plastic or cellophane tubing, found at most craft stores, or use your own cellophane—lightly tinted so it is easy to see through. Put the model into the tubing, then section off each model by tying the tube with pieces of ribbon; position the models so none are upside-down when the ends of the tube are tied together. You may wish to include candies or little gifts in the tube with your models.

Many of the models can be fastened to flower to candy leis with thread, ribbon, or thin, soft wire. It is also possible to string several of the models, such as the star and the rose, together into leis without puncturing the bills.

Government Property

Please remember that all U.S. currency, even that in your possession, is government property. While it is legal to fold money, it is illegal to intentionally destroy it by gluing, cutting, or tearing in any manner.

Foreign Currency

These money folds are designed for U.S. currency, with proportions (ratio of width to length) based on those of the one dollar bill; check *Paper Substitutions* for a list of acceptable sizes. The amount of leeway on the dimensions, or whether an unrelated size can be used, should be considered an experiment. Keep in mind that an unspecified dimension may work for one model but not for another.

Paper Substitutions

(Note: If you want to avoid the hows and whys, calculated paper sizes are offered below in red. I advise you not to round off these figures but to use them as they are.)

To use paper in place of money and achieve the proper result, your paper must be either the same size as a dollar, which is approximately 2 5/8" x 6 1/8", it must have the same ratio of width to length as a dollar. The *width:length* of a dollar can be calculated to .75 :1.75 and then expanded by multiplying both numbers by the same number (*N*).

$$N = \text{number}$$
$$.75 \times N : 1.75 \times N$$

This equation provides the following paper sizes:

1 1/2 x 3 1/2 (eg., *N*=2)
2 1/4 x 5 1/4
3 x 7
3 3/4 x 8 3/4
4 1/2 x 10 1/2
5 1/4 x 12 1/4
6 x 14

Apply these dimensions in any unit of measurement (inch, centimeter, etc.).
Use the equation above to calculate more sizes if needed.

If you have a standard paper size, such as 8 1/2"x 11" (letter size) or 6" (origami paper), that you want to use as an established length, calculate the unknown width by dividing the length by 2.33.

$$\text{Length} \div 2.33 = \text{Width}$$

Round off your result to the nearest 1/8 (bills actually vary in size that much). Calculated sizes using the lengths mentioned are in inches:

2 1/2 x 6
3 5/8 x 8 1/2
4 3/4 x 11

Important:

Before you cut paper for a particular model, read the information that precedes the model's instructions. It will note whether the model requires paper with sides that are the same or at least similar in color. Several money models do display both sides of the paper, which may not be evident in the examples.

Color-Coded Instructions

The colors red and blue are used to highlight instructional arrows and lines, offering the following advantages:

❋ Fold arrows and lines are easily distinguished from edges and creases.

❋ In folds that have more than one instructional arrow and line, such as the combination fold below, colors are used to correlate the different arrows and lines with the written instructions. The colors also designate the order in which the folds are made. In general: red before blue; blue before black.

Rabbit ear fold.
1. Fold edges in on creases.
2. Fold sides together.
3. Mountain fold is set by folding new flap down.

As seen, employing different colors makes it possible to easily explain combination folds in a model's instructions.

❋ Unrelated instructions of a two-part step are clearly defined by the different colors. As a rule, A is red and B is blue.

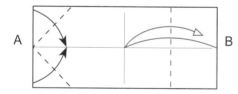

A. Fold edges to center.
B. Fold edge to crease; unfold.

For the few instructions with three parts, black is used as the third color.

❋ The colors are also used to identify notable edges and creases and to correlate them with the written instructions. See the example on the following page.

The Fundamentals of Origami

Steps

- Steps are numbered. Follow the instructions step by step. Do not skip any steps.
- Each step contains a diagram and written instructions that show and tell you what to do. To help understand an instruction, look at the next step to see the result.
- An intermediate step may also follow an instruction to show how to accomplish the required fold. An intermediate step is labeled with a number and a lower case letter.

Be Precise

- Take your time and be as precise as possible. Press hard (especially when folding money) to make sharp creases.
- Match and fold all pertinent edges, creases, and points of a fold exactly together.
- Align center lines when they pertain to a fold. A center line is a crease that runs through the center of your paper, model, or a section thereof.

Align center lines to fold accurately.

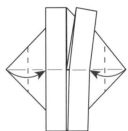

Drawings

- Instructional drawings do not always depict edges and folds perfectly aligned as they actually should be. This is in order to show existing folds and layers. In the example above, the left side is properly aligned while the right side is shown askew, exhibiting folds and layers.
- Drawings may be enlarged to clarify instructions. Significant enlargements are noted by the letter *E*.
- When a section of a drawing is outlined with a box, only that section is magnified and shown in the following steps.

The Key to Folds, Lines and Arrows

The Different Lines

——————— **Edge**   - - - - - - - - **Fold**

——————— **Crease**   —·—·—·—·—·. **Mtn. Fold**
                                                  (mountain fold)

·············· **Unseen Edge / Unseen Fold / Guide**

Sections of edge lines are occasionally highlighted with color. The color of the all other lines may vary between red, blue, and black.

Simple Folds and Arrows

Arrows vary in color and size. Fold arrows also greatly vary in shape.

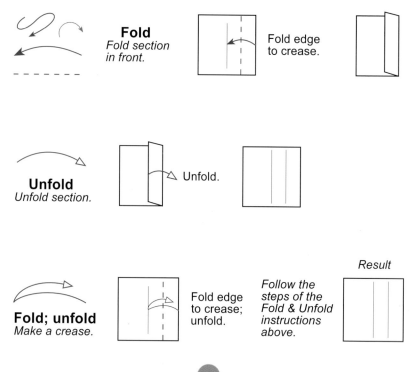

Fold
Fold section in front.

Fold edge to crease.

Unfold
Unfold section.

Unfold.

Fold; unfold
Make a crease.

Fold edge to crease; unfold.

Follow the steps of the Fold & Unfold instructions above.

Result

The Key to Folds, Lines, and Arrows

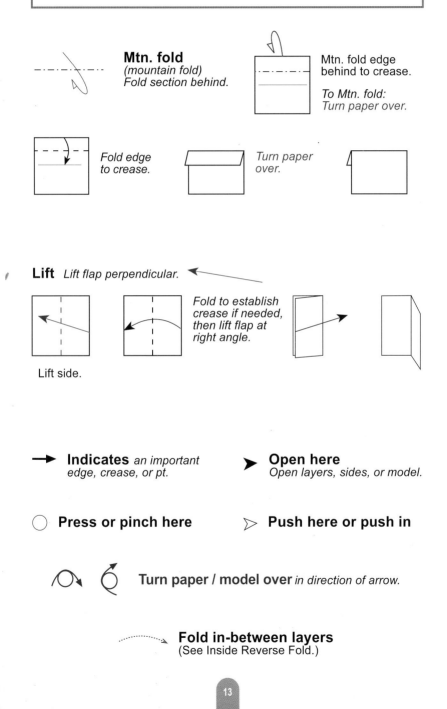

Mtn. fold
(mountain fold)
Fold section behind.

Mtn. fold edge
behind to crease.

To Mtn. fold:
Turn paper over.

Fold edge
to crease.

Turn paper
over.

Lift *Lift flap perpendicular.*

Fold to establish
crease if needed,
then lift flap at
right angle.

Lift side.

Indicates *an important*
edge, crease, or pt.

Open here
Open layers, sides, or model.

Press or pinch here

Push here or push in

Turn paper / model over *in direction of arrow.*

Fold in-between layers
(See Inside Reverse Fold.)

Combination Folds

A *combination fold* combines two or more folds into a single step. These folds are made in a specific order, referred to as a folding procedure. The folding procedure is listed for all *combination folds*, as they are applied in the model instructions.

The *squash fold* and the *inside reverse fold*, which are the two most common *combination folds*, are explained here in greater detail to help you accomplish them accurately.

The Squash Fold

Example:

Squash fold.
1. Establish fold between corner pts. on flap. Lift section perpendicular.
2. Open layers.
3. Flatten section symmetrically.

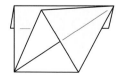

To accurately accomplish the squash fold:

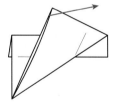

1. To establish fold:
align all edges exactly. Fold section over between corner pts. as shown.

Lift flap up at right angle.

2. To open layers:
Insert your finger up to pt.
Smooth down folded edge.

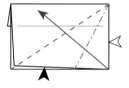

3. To flatten symmetrically:
Match indicated edges & pts. of layers.
Hold fold firmly in place. Align edge on fold beneath. Flatten section.

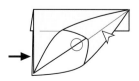

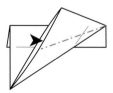

The Inside Reverse Fold

Example:

Inside reverse fold.
1. Establish creases: fold corner to edge; unfold.
2. Open sides.
3. Fold corner in on creases.

To accurately accomplish the inside reverse fold:

1. To establish creases: use the inside reverse fold arrow ········⟍ to show you where to fold an edge or pt. Align edges exactly & keep aligned as you fold corner to edge as shown; unfold.

(Note: It can be difficult to accurately crease two layers at once. Minor adjustments are easily made in the steps that follow.)

2. Open sides as shown.
3. To fold corner in on creases, push on edge to fold corner in on back crease first.

To continue:
Mtn. fold crease, pinching sides together to create a flap. Make a precise pt. Match edges.

(Note: Edge is now a crease. Pt. comes to exact pt. and edges match perfectly.)

Fold flap over to complete fold.

Plumeria (Melia)

Plumeria

Use the back of a one dollar bill or any larger denomination bill with an old design. Select a bill with a back border of even width. (The border is used to create the slender petals of a plumeria flower.) Paper substitutions are fine, but the effect of plumeria petals will be lost. The *Plumeria* displays one side of the paper.

The drawings depict the border of the bill when it pertains to the petal design. Begin with the desired side or back of bill down.

1. Fold in half; unfold.

2. Fold edges to center line.

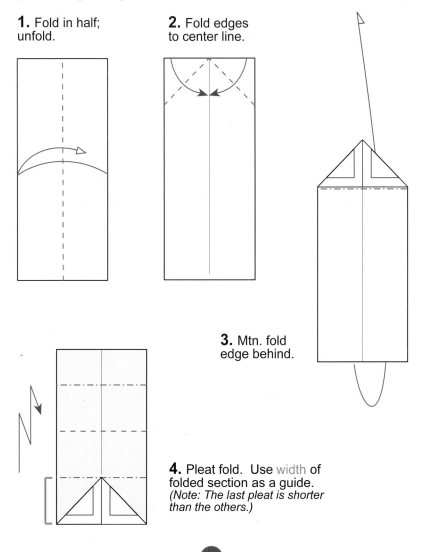

3. Mtn. fold edge behind.

4. Pleat fold. Use width of folded section as a guide.
(Note: The last pleat is shorter than the others.)

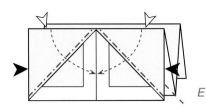

5. Inside reverse fold both ends. (See 5a & 5b.)

E

5a. Fold pt. to pt. Flatten section symmetrically.

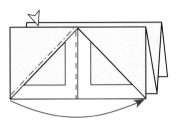

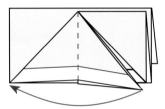

5b. Fold new flap back over. Repeat steps 5a & 5b on right.

6. Squash fold end sections of both flaps. (See 6a.)

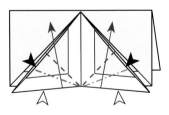

6a. On each side:
1. Fold flap in half. Lift end section perpendicular.
2. Open sides. ◄
3. Flatten symmetrically. ▷

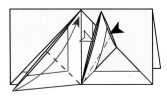

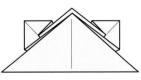

Back View of Result

7. Unfold flap from behind.

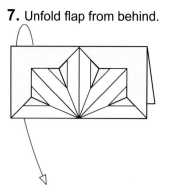

8. Fold edges to center line.

9. Fold in half.

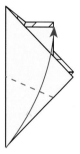

10. Fold pt. to pt.

11. Mtn. fold tip in-between layers. Temporarily hold with a paper clip to set fold.

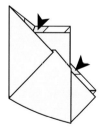

12. Open model. Slightly bend or curl ends of petals.

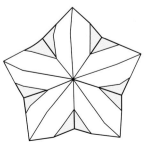

Star *(Hōkū)*

Star

Use the back of any bill. Have on hand a pointed metal nail file or similar object. Paper substitutions: the *Star* displays one side of the paper.

1. Begin with the desired side or back of bill down. Fold in half; unfold.

2. Fold edges to center.

3. Fold in half.

In the following steps, you will be folding a pentagon with sides that are just slightly longer than the width of the strip.

4. Fold corner up.

Width

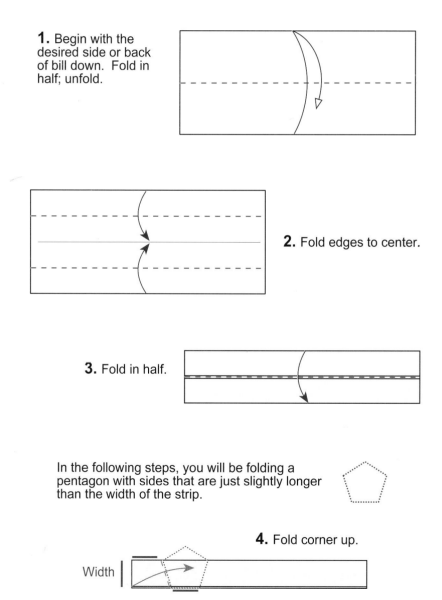

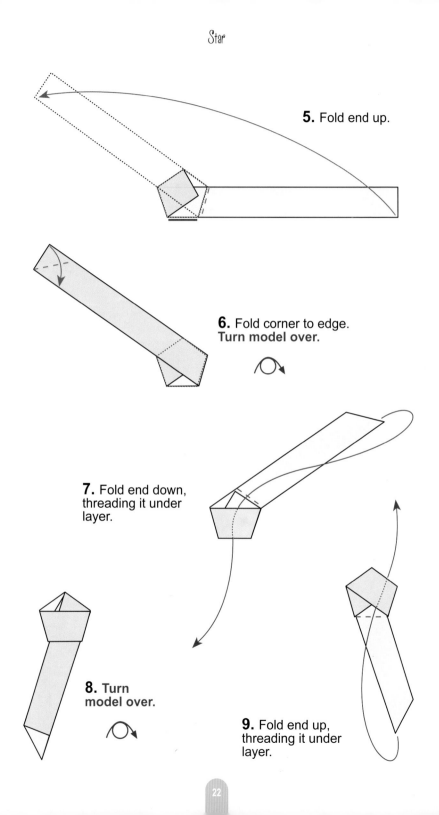

5. Fold end up.

6. Fold corner to edge.
Turn model over.

7. Fold end down,
threading it under
layer.

**8. Turn
model over.**

9. Fold end up,
threading it under
layer.

E

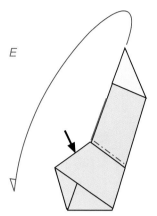

10. Mtn. fold end behind. Align edge on indicated edge.

11. Fold end under top layers (darker shade).

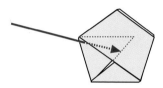

12. With a pointed metal nail file or other object, push on edge, unrolling fold beneath top layers.

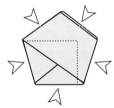

13. Push mid-pt. of sides in. Use a pointed object to lift layers & to form pts.

Owl (Pueo)

Owl

Use the back of a one dollar bill for best results. Select a bill with thin and even front borders. The four corners of the front borders are used to create the *Owl's* eyes; the border is also used to create a contrasting beak. (Take this in to account when substituting paper; select paper with sides in contrasting color.)

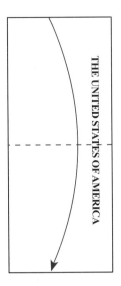

The drawings depict the border of the bill when it pertains to the design.

1. Begin with back of bill down & bill positioned as shown. Fold in half.

2. Fold in half; unfold.

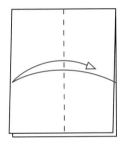

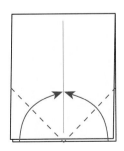

3. Fold edges to center.

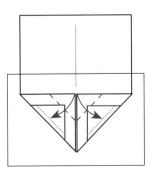

4. Fold each corner pt. to pt. as shown.

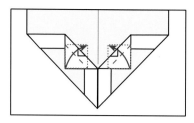

5. Fold corner pt. of top layer up on both sides.

6.
A. On each side: minutely adjust flaps to best shaped eyes within the white borders. Do not overlap indicated ear.
B. Fold pt. up.

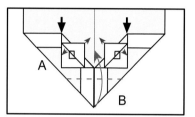

7. Fold tip down to create beak.

8. Mtn. fold flap down behind.
(Note: Borders are not folded.)

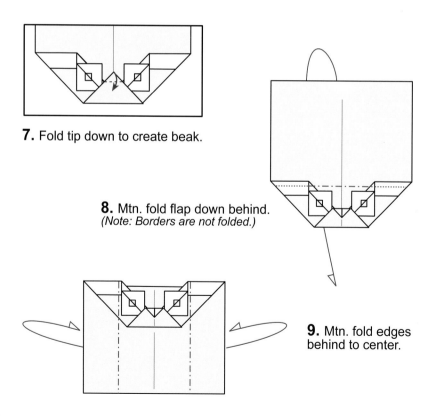

9. Mtn. fold edges behind to center.

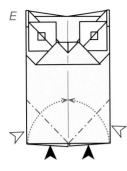

E

10. Inside reverse fold both sides.
1. Establish creases: fold corner
to center; unfold.
2. Open sides.
3. Fold corner in on creases.

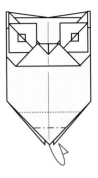

11. Mtn. fold pt. in.

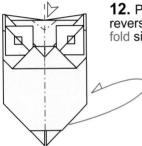

12. Push on edge to
reverse fold in as you
fold sides together.

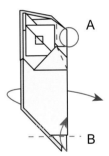

A

B

13.
A. Pinch edge as
you fold open sides.
B. Fold both feet up.

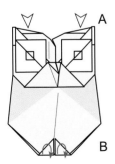

A

B

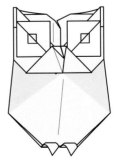

14.
A. Push on edges
to round.
B. Curl feet down.

Turtle *(Honu)*

Turtle

Use any of the following: the front of a one dollar bill, either side of any larger bill with an old design, or the back of any larger bill with a current design. Paper substitutions: paper with contrasting sides may be acceptable; see final instructional drawing to determine if your selection is suitable.

1. Begin with the intended side/design of shell down. Fold in half; unfold. Repeat.

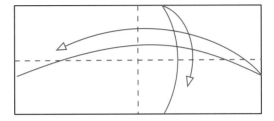

2. Fold edge to center; unfold. Repeat.

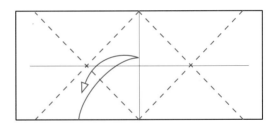

3. Rabbit ear fold each side.
1. Refold edges up on creases as you fold sides together.
2. Mtn. fold is set by folding new flap down.

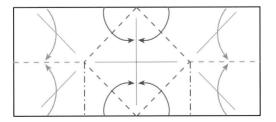

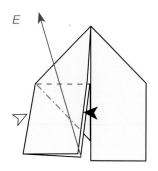

4. Squash fold flap.
1. Establish fold: fold flap up.
Lift flap perpendicular.
2. Open layers.
3. Flatten section on creases.

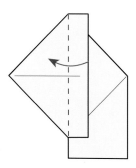

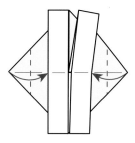

5. Fold edge out from center line. Repeat steps 4 & 5 on right.

6. Fold corner pts. in.

Check that back design is upright before proceeding.

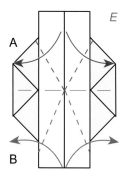

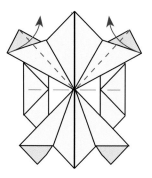

7. On both sides:
A. Fold edge to corner pt.
B. Fold corner pt. up & out.

8. Fold corner pts. up.

9. On each side:
A. Pinch tip. Lift to separate layers, unhooking fold from pleat beneath. (See right side.)
B. Hold layer down near center. Fold flap down on crease. Flatten.

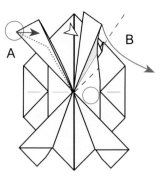

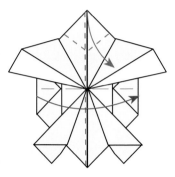

10. Fold sides together to reverse fold section in.

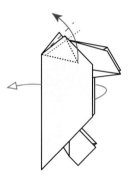

11. Reverse fold head out as you unfold sides. Do not completely unfold.

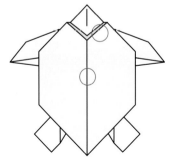

12. Pinch overlap & ridge to further define shell.

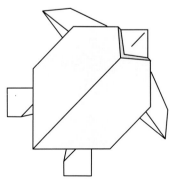

Coconut Frond Fish

Coconut Frond Fish

Use the back of any two bills. Have on hand a toothpick or similar object. This model borrows the technique of weaving two coconut fronds into a fish. Paper substitutions: the *Coconut Frond Fish* displays one side of the paper.

1. Begin with the desired side or back of bill down. Fold in half; unfold.

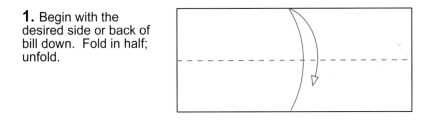

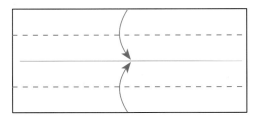

2. Fold edges to center.

3. Fold corners to center.

4. Fold each corner almost to center, allowing for thickness of later fold.

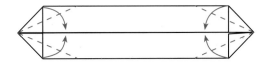

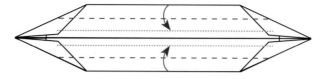

5. For slightly shorter fins & tail, fold edges to pts. shown. For longer fins & tail, fold edges to center.

6. Fold in half. Set folds. Repeat steps 1 to 6 on second bill.

7. Fold first strip as shown.

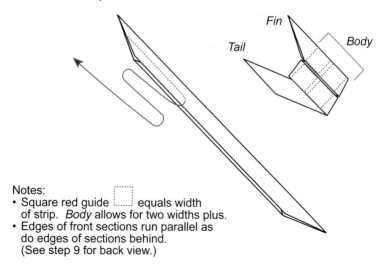

Notes:
- Square red guide ⬚ equals width of strip. *Body* allows for two widths plus.
- Edges of front sections run parallel as do edges of sections behind. (See step 9 for back view.)

8. Insert second strip under section as shown. **Turn model over** to mtn. fold end behind, weaving it under indicated section behind.

Steps 9 & 10
Turn model over to mtn. fold end behind, weaving it under indicated section.

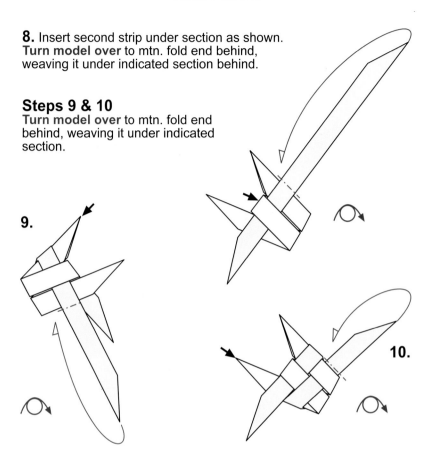

9.

10.

11. Pull on fins only if you wish to lengthen them. Pull on tail sections to tighten weave. Use a toothpick to lift and arrange plaits. Curl or twist fins & tail sections to shape. Optional: simultaneously push on sides to add dimension.

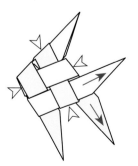

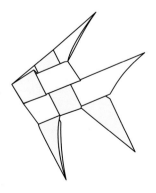

The Luckiest Frog

The Luckiest Frog

Use the back of a one dollar bill for best results. It provides the necessary color for a green frog. Paper substitution: select paper with sides of the same or similar color.

1. Begin with the desired side or back of bill up. Fold in half; unfold.

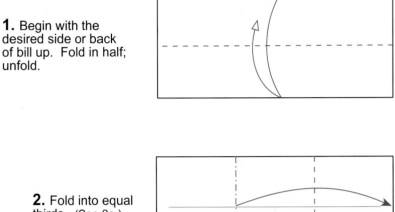

2. Fold into equal thirds. (See 2a.)

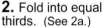
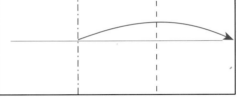

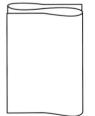

2a.
1. Fold without creasing.
2. Adjust into equal thirds, aligning top edges first.
3. Set folds.

Model is rotated.

3. Fold corners to center; unfold.

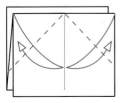

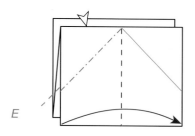

E

4. Fold corner to corner.
Flatten section on creases.

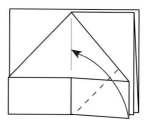

5. Fold corner to center.

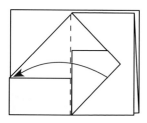

6. Fold flap back.

7. Repeat steps 4 (shown) to 6.

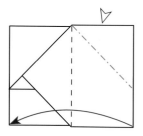

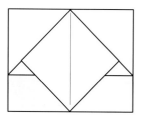

8. Turn model over.

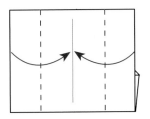

9. Fold sides in.

10. Inside reverse fold each corner.
1. Establish creases:
fold corner to center; unfold.
2. Open sides.
3. Fold corner in on creases.

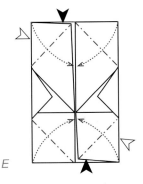

E

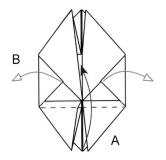

B

A

11.
A. Fold middle flap up.
B. Unfold side flaps.

12.
A. Pinch flaps. Fold straight out.
B. Fold pt. up on back border of bill.

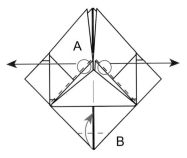

A

B

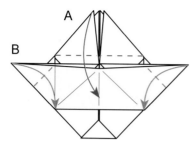

13. On both sides:
A. Fold flap down.
B. Fold pt. to corner.

14.
A. Fold flaps in half.
B. Fold pt. up on each side.

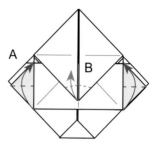

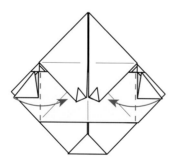

15. Fold legs in.

16. Refold flaps into
hidden pockets beneath.

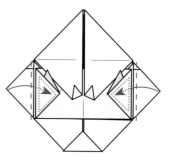

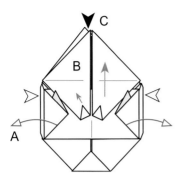

17.
A. Partially unfold back legs, angling them inward.
B. Lift front feet perpendicular then lift front legs.
C. Push on sides & insert finger between layers to open mouth & to slightly round frog's back.

Turn model over.

Insert a lucky penny or gold dollar in the mouth of your frog.

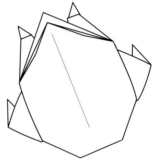

Seashell _(Pūpū)_

Seashell

Use the back of a one dollar bill or any larger denomination bill with an old design. Have on hand a pencil or similar object. Paper substitutions: select paper with sides of similar or contrasting colors. (Note: instructions offer the design options seen in the examples.)

1. Begin with the desired side or back of bill down & bill upside down. Fold in half; unfold.

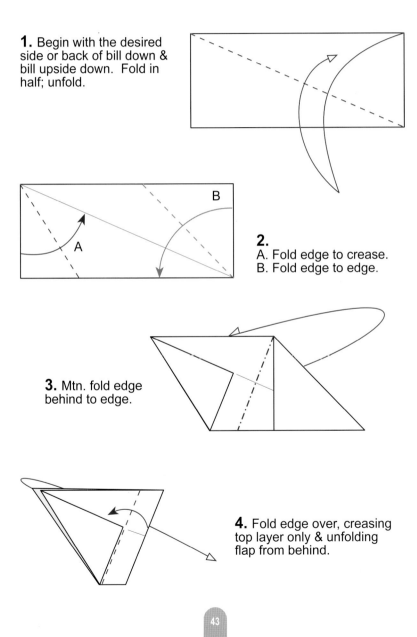

2.
A. Fold edge to crease.
B. Fold edge to edge.

3. Mtn. fold edge behind to edge.

4. Fold edge over, creasing top layer only & unfolding flap from behind.

Model is rotated.

5. Fold pt. to pt. on crease.

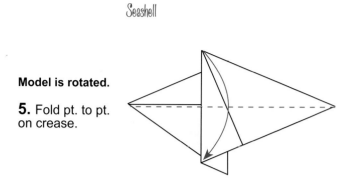

6. Determine desired number of segments. Pleat fold accordingly. To begin: Mtn. fold pt. behind then fold forward. (See 6a.) Repeat.

Examples

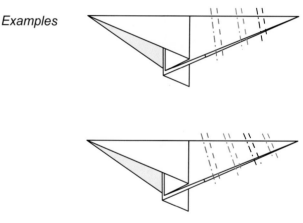

6a.

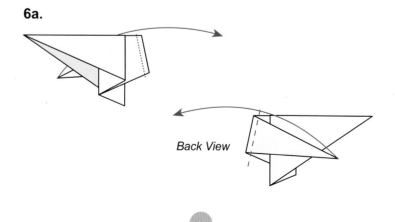

Back View

7. Set creases well. Unfold sides.

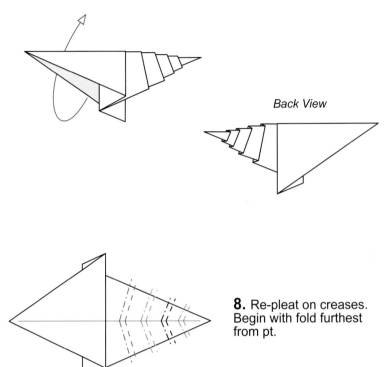

Back View

8. Re-pleat on creases. Begin with fold furthest from pt.

Steps 9 & 10 are optional.
(Skip these steps if a long shell is preferred.)

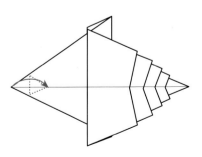

9. To crop tip of shell:
Turn model over. Fold tip in.

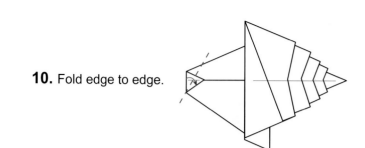

10. Fold edge to edge.

11. Refold sides together.

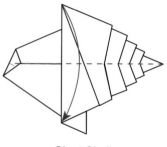

Short Shell

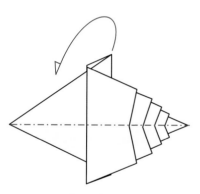

Long Shell

12. Adjust pleats. Fold
tab under top layer.

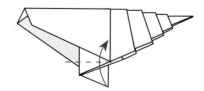

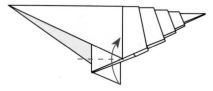

13.
A. Fold edge up.
B. Insert a pencil & push on edges to round shell.

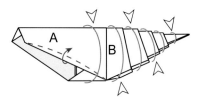

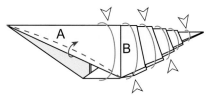

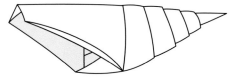

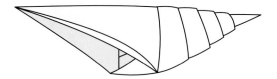

Flower (Pua)

Flower

Use the back of any bill. Have on hand a toothpick or similar object. Paper substitutions: consider that the front of this model displays one side of the paper and that the back displays both sides; select paper accordingly.

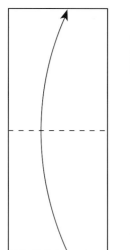

1. Begin with the desired side or back of bill down. Fold in half.

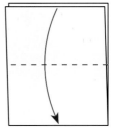

2. Fold edge to edge. Repeat behind.

3. Fold edge to edge. Repeat behind.

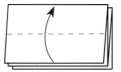

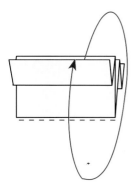

4. Fold back section in front.

5. Fold sections in half.

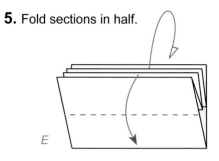

E

6. Inside reverse fold both ends of all flaps.
1. Establish creases on outer flaps: fold corner to edge; unfold.
2. Open sides.
3. Fold corner in on creases.
On middle flaps, fold corner in, matching folds of outer flap.

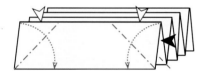

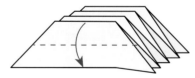

7. Fold edge to edge.

8. Fold flap down.

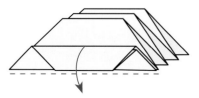

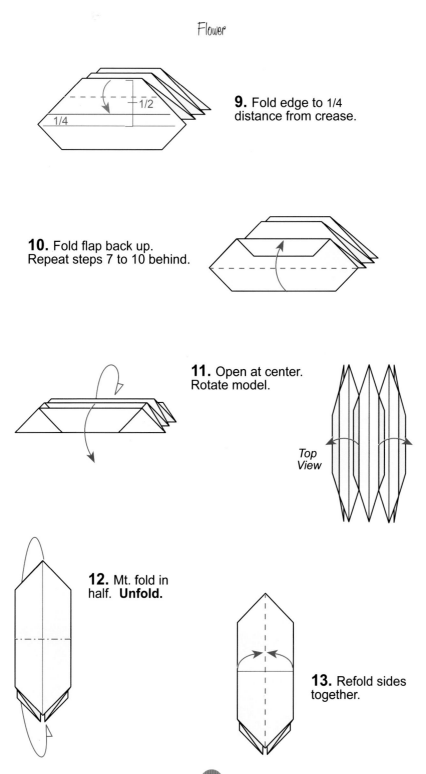

9. Fold edge to 1/4 distance from crease.

10. Fold flap back up. Repeat steps 7 to 10 behind.

11. Open at center. Rotate model.

Top View

12. Mt. fold in half. **Unfold.**

13. Refold sides together.

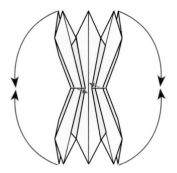

14. Fold sides together on creases to fan out petals. Slightly or greatly offset folds at center to determine style. (See example.)

15. Pinch edges between all petals. Shape petals. **Turn model over.**

Complete steps 16 & 17 on left side first, then repeat on right side.

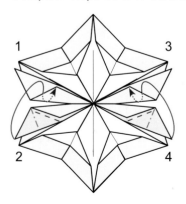

16. Pinch petals 1 & 2 together from beneath. Use a toothpick to fold flap (darker shade) between layers. Push on center of flap, folding it in half between layers.

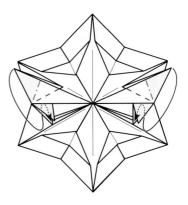

17. Use a toothpick to fold flap in between lower petal & center flap. Push on center of flap, folding it in half between layers.

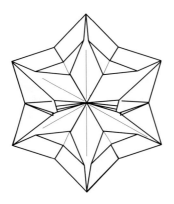

18. Turn model over.

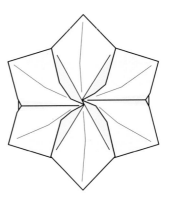

Pineapple *(Hala kahiki)*

Pineapple

Use the back of any bill larger than one dollar. Bills with an old design provide more color for the best results. Paper substitutions: the *Pineapple* displays one side of the paper.

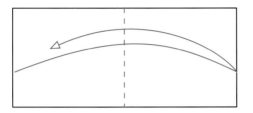

1. Begin with the desired side or back of bill down. Fold in half; unfold.

2. Fold edges to center.

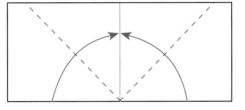

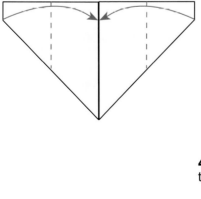

3. Fold edges to center.

4. Fold edges to center.

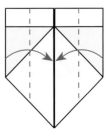

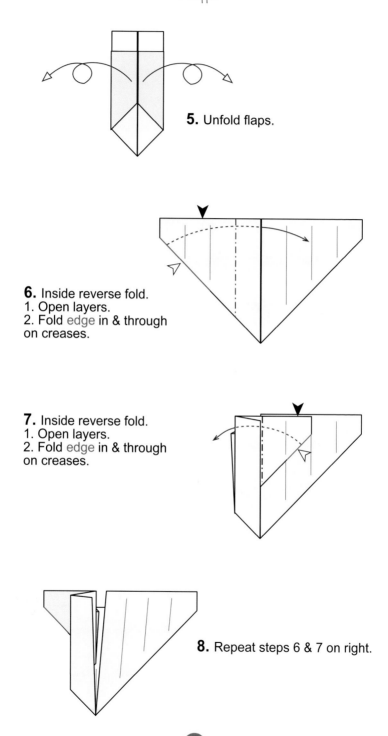

5. Unfold flaps.

6. Inside reverse fold.
1. Open layers.
2. Fold edge in & through on creases.

7. Inside reverse fold.
1. Open layers.
2. Fold edge in & through on creases.

8. Repeat steps 6 & 7 on right.

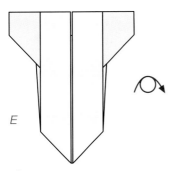

E

9. Turn model over.

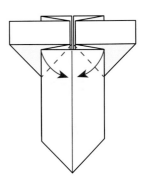

10. Fold edges to center.

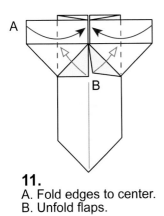

A

B

11.
A. Fold edges to center.
B. Unfold flaps.

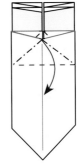

12. Fold mid-pt. down & edges to center on creases.

13. Inside reverse fold all flaps.
1. Establish creases: fold corner to center; unfold.
2. Open layers.
3. Fold corner in on creases.

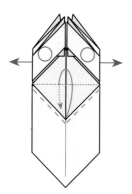

14. Pinch all layers & pull sides out to refold pt. in on creases. (See 14a.)

14a.

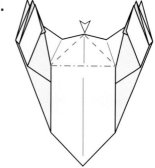

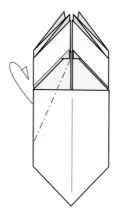

15. Turn model over to fold edge to center.

B

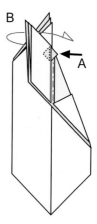

A

16.
A. Fold indicated tab in between layers.
B. Mtn. fold flaps, wrapping them tightly back behind.
Repeat steps 15 & 16 on left.

17. Fold tip up on bill's border. Set folds very well before proceeding. (Temporarily use a paper clip or place a weight on model to compress.)

Turn model over.

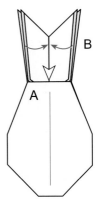

18.
A. Push on edge to round.
B. Fan out crown.

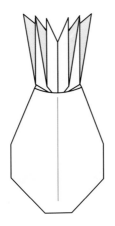

Aloha Shirt

Aloha Shirt

Use a one or twenty dollar bill with an old design. Have on hand a toothpick or similar object. Paper substitutions: select paper with sides of the same color.

1. Begin with back of bill or side intended as *shirt's* front down. Fold in half; unfold.

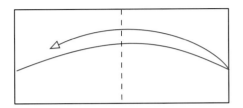

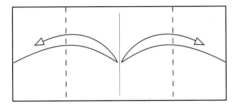

2. Fold edges to center; unfold.

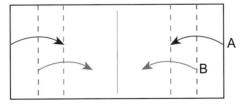

3. On both sides:
A. Fold edge to crease.
B. Refold new edge in on crease.

4. Mtn. fold edges behind to center.

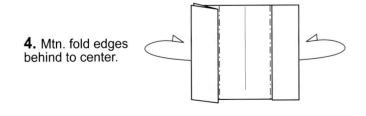

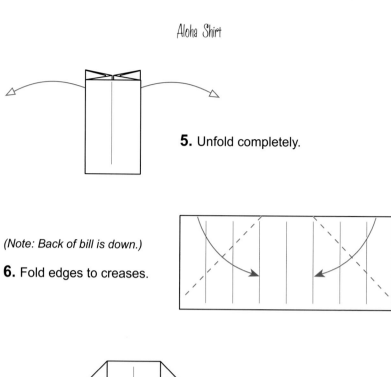

5. Unfold completely.

(Note: Back of bill is down.)

6. Fold edges to creases.

7. Mtn. fold edges behind to center. Unfold completely.

Complete steps 8 to 10 on one side first, then repeat on other side.

8.
1. Define creases & their pts. of intersection.
2. Fold corner in half.
3. Fold edges in on creases.
(Note: Mtn. folds are set in step 9.)

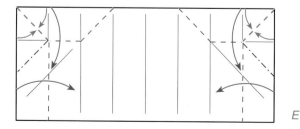

E

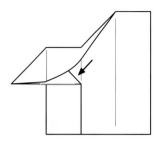

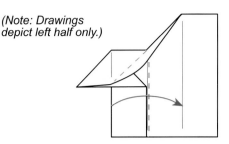

(Note: Drawings depict left half only.)

9. Align crease on edge. Run edge parallel to lower edge. Set indicated fold.

10. Fold side in on crease. Fold is made in process.

11.
A. Fold edge down. Fold new edge to pt. above shoulder of shirt.
B. Fold pt. of each sleeve up as seen on right. Unfold.

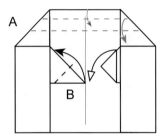

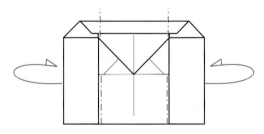

12. Mtn. fold edges behind to center on creases.

13.
A. Inside reverse fold sleeves.
    1. Open layers.
    2. Fold edge in on creases.
B. Fold corner down.

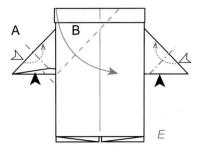

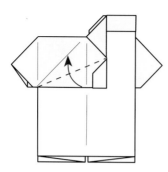

14. Fold edge to crease.

15. Fold flap up. Repeat steps 13B to 15 on right.

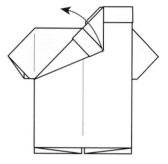

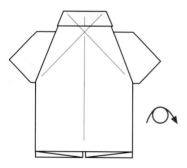

16. Turn model over.

17. Open side to fold flap down. Repeat on right. (Right side will overlap left.)

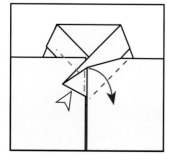

18. Fold corner down. Push on edge to flatten section. Repeat on left.

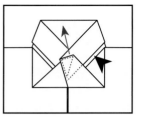

(Note: All drawings show right overlapping left.)

19. Lift hidden edge of collar & gently stretch up.

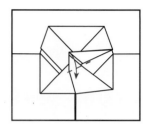

20. Fold edge of collar down. Repeat steps 19 & 20 on left.

21. On each side: Use a toothpick to lift collar. Push on edge to splay & shape collar.

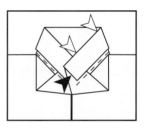

Humuhumunukunukuāpuaʻa
(Hawaiʻi State Fish)

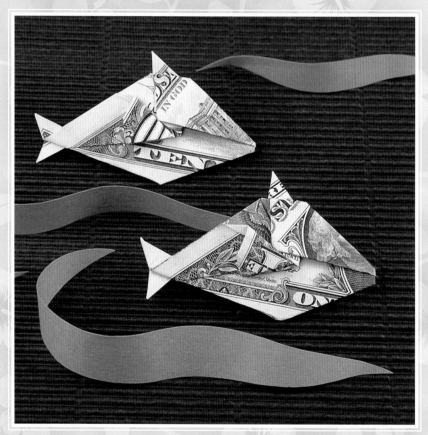

Humuhumunukunukuāpua'a

Use the back of any bill; use the front of any bill except a redesigned bill. Have handy a toothpick or similar object. Paper substitutions: select paper with sides of the same color.

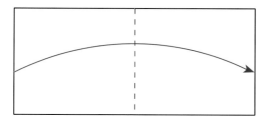

1. Begin with the desired side down. Fold in half.

2. Fold in half; unfold.

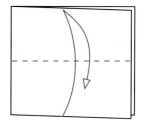

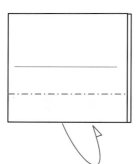

3. Mtn. fold edge behind to crease.

4. Squash fold.
1. Establish fold between corner pts. on flap. Lift section perpendicular.
2. Open layers.
3. Flatten section symmetrically.

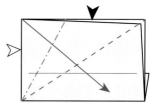

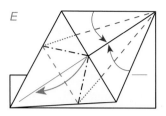

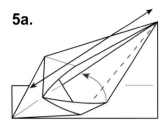

5. Petal fold.
1. Establish creases: fold edges to center; unfold.
2. Fold center pt. up between crease pts.
3. Fold edges in. Gently stretch to align on center. (See 5a.)

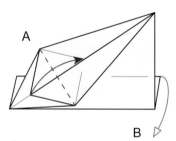

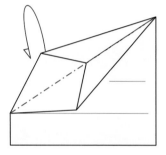

6.
A. Fold flap up.
B. Unfold flap from behind.

7. Mtn. fold flap behind on crease

8. Fold both flaps up.

9. Fold corner to corner on creases. Flatten. (See 9a.) Repeat behind.

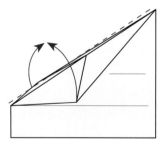

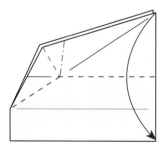

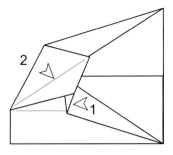

9a.
1. Push in here.
2. Push down here.

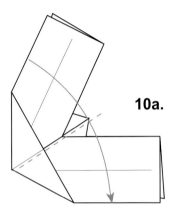

10a.

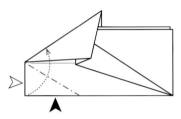

10. Inside reverse fold.
1. Establish creases: fold corner to edge; unfold.
2. Fold side open as seen in 10a.
3. Flatten section on creases.
4. Fold side down.

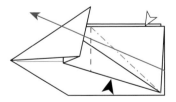

11. Squash fold.
1. Establish fold. (See 11a.)
2. Establish creases: fold between crease pt. & corner pt.
3. Lift flap perpendicular.
4. Open layers.
5. Flatten section on creases

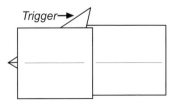

Trigger→

11a.
(Note: Position of fold to trigger.)
Fold flap as shown. Unfold.

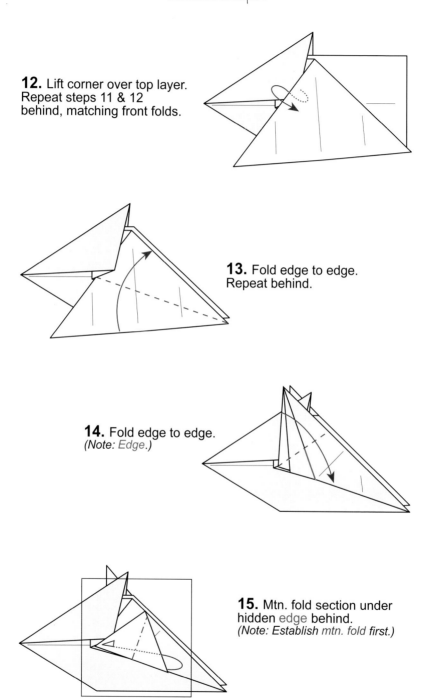

12. Lift corner over top layer. Repeat steps 11 & 12 behind, matching front folds.

13. Fold edge to edge. Repeat behind.

14. Fold edge to edge. *(Note: Edge.)*

15. Mtn. fold section under hidden edge behind. *(Note: Establish mtn. fold first.)*

16. Inside reverse fold end of fin.
1. Open layers.
2. Push edge in.
Repeat steps 14 to 16 behind.

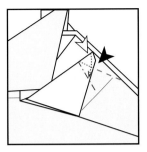

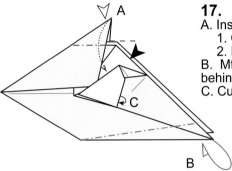

17.
A. Inside reverse fold trigger.
   1. Open sides.
   2. Fold section in along edges.
B. Mtn. fold edge under. Repeat behind. Match front fold.
C. Curl edge of both fins outward.

18.
A. Fold trigger back up slightly below edges.
B. Mtn. fold flap in & down.
C. Inside reverse fold pt. to form mouth.

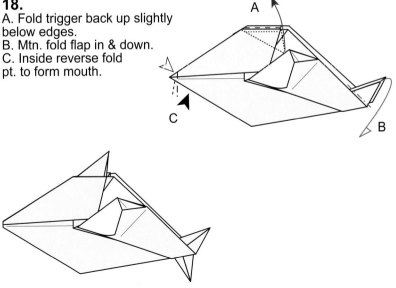

'Ukulele

ʻUkulele

Use the front of a one dollar bill. Note the circular emblem that represents the hole in the *ʻUkulele* in the examples - select a bill that has a centered emblem. (To check, fold your bill in half as in step 1.) Have on hand a toothpick or similar object. Instructions use the emblem and the words printed on the dollar as reference points for folds. To use higher denominations (old designs only), you will need to create these folds proportionately; paper substitutions are not recommended.

1. Begin with front of bill down & bill upside down.
A. Fold in half; unfold.
B. Fold edge in on front border of bill.

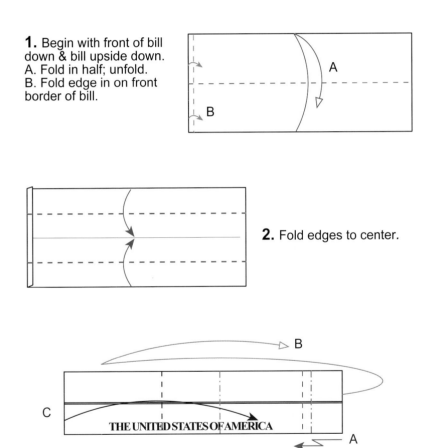

2. Fold edges to center.

3.
A. Pleat fold. Establish mtn. fold first. Fold new edge up to last A in AMERICA.
B. Mtn. fold edge behind; unfold. Fold is made after last S in STATES.
C. Fold edge up to E in AMERICA.

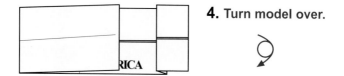

4. Turn model over.

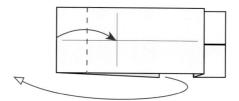

5. Fold edge to crease, creasing top layer only & unfolding flap from behind. Crease especially well.

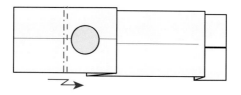

6. Pleat fold. Establish mtn. fold first then fold new edge up to edge of emblem. *(Note: Create the smallest pleat possible.)*

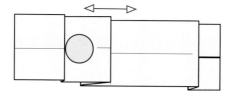

7. Unfold center pleat.

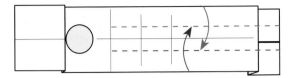

8. Fold into equal thirds. Unfold

A

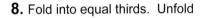

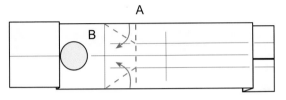

9.
A. Reestablish crease.
B. Fold; unfold each edge in.

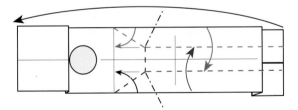

10. Refold edges up on creases in the order of red, blue, black.
Folds are completed simultaneously when flap is folded over.

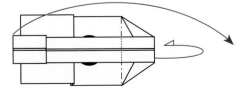

11. Mtn. fold only edge
behind on crease, folding
flap over.

Model is rotated.

12.
A. Mtn. fold edges behind.
B. Tuck indicated pleat under pleat beneath. Use a toothpick.

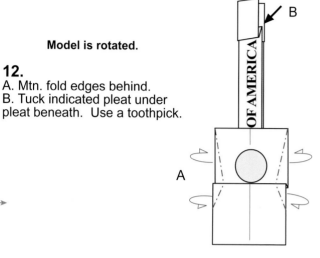

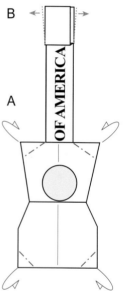

13.
A. Mtn. fold corners behind.
B. Angle sides of top layer out.
(See back view of result below.)

14.
A. Clip corners: mtn. fold behind.
B. Push sides in to slightly

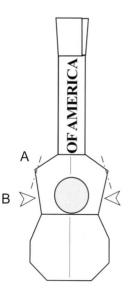

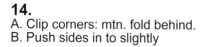

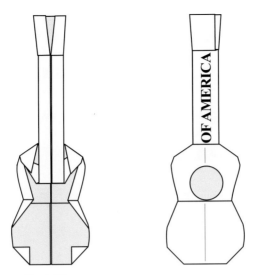

Back View

Gecko (Mo'o)

Gecko

Use the back of any bill for interesting but green geckos. Use the front of all bills except those of current design for truer-to-color but less interesting geckos. Paper substitutions: the *Gecko* displays one side of the paper.

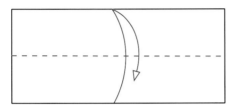

1. Begin with the desired side down. Fold in half; unfold.

2. Mtn. fold in half; unfold.

3.
A. Fold edges to center.
B. Fold edge to crease; unfold.

4.
A. Fold edges to center.
B. Mtn. fold edge behind to crease.

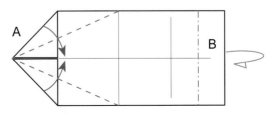

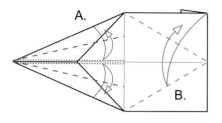

5.
A. Fold edges almost to center.
Crease as shown. Unfold.
B. Fold; unfold each corner in.

6.
A. Fold; unfold each edge
to center.
B. Unfold flap from behind.

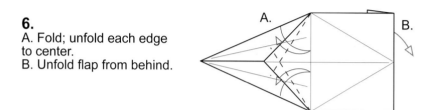

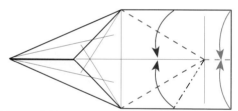

7. Rabbit ear fold.
1. Refold edges up on creases as you fold sides together.
2. Mtn. fold is set by folding new flap down.

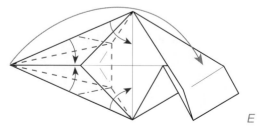

E

8.
1. Refold edges in on creases. Define intersection pts. of creases.
2. Fold pt. down. Align center lines.
3. Flatten to set mtn. folds.

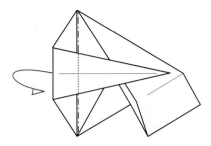

9. Mtn. fold edge behind on crease.

10. Fold side open on center line. Flatten section symmetrically.

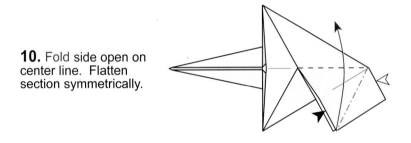

11. Squash fold flap.
1. Establish crease. (See 11a.)
2. Lift flap perpendicular.
3. Open layers
4. Flatten on creases.

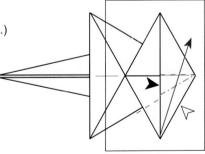

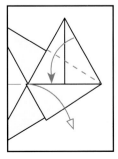

11a. Fold flap in half; unfold.

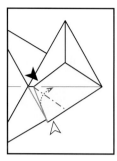

12. Inside reverse fold.
Lift flap to fold edges to center.

13. Fold flap down.

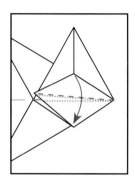

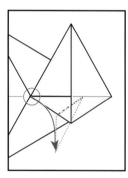

14. Pinch tip. Fold flap out -
fold is made partially beneath
top layer. Stretch gently to
maximize length. Flatten new
overlapping section. Repeat
steps 11 to 14 on opposite side.

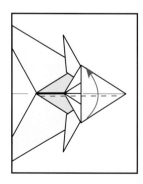

15. Fold flap up.

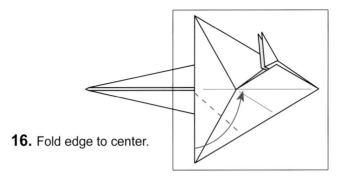

16. Fold edge to center.

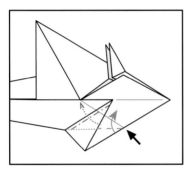

17. Inside reverse fold.
1. Mtn. fold edge behind.
2. Fold side in.
(Note: Indicated pt.)

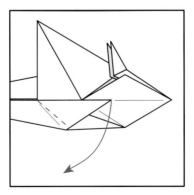

18. Fold flap out & down. Make fold very close to crease. Stretch gently to maximize length. Flatten new overlapping section.

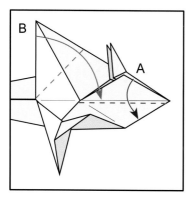

19.
A. Fold front legs down.
B. Repeat steps 16 (shown)
to 18 on opposite side.

20. Fold model in half.

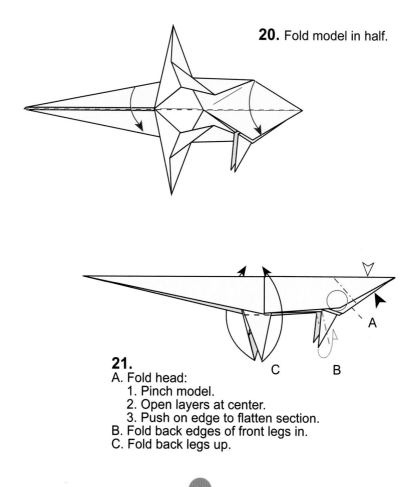

21.
A. Fold head:
    1. Pinch model.
    2. Open layers at center.
    3. Push on edge to flatten section.
B. Fold back edges of front legs in.
C. Fold back legs up.

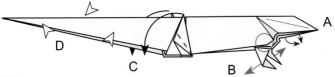

22.
A. Pinch sides as shown. Separate bottom layer on each side of head & fold together.
B. Fold front legs straight out.
C. Fold back legs down.
D. Curl tail.

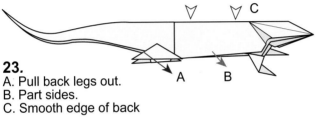

23.
A. Pull back legs out.
B. Part sides.
C. Smooth edge of back

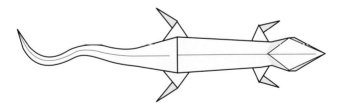

Slipper / Other Slipper
(Kāmaʻa pale wāwae)

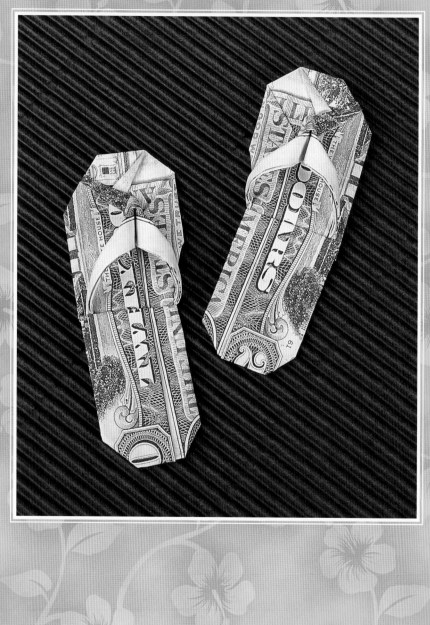

Slipper

Use the back of any bill except the redesigned five dollar bill, which lacks color. Select a bill with a border of even width. Several folds in the *Slipper* are based on the width of the border; the border is also used create the strap, contrasting it in color from the rest of the model. Paper substitutions: reproduce the folds proportionately that involve the border of the bill. The *Slipper* displays one side of the paper. *(Note: for a pair of slippers, you will need two identical bills.)*

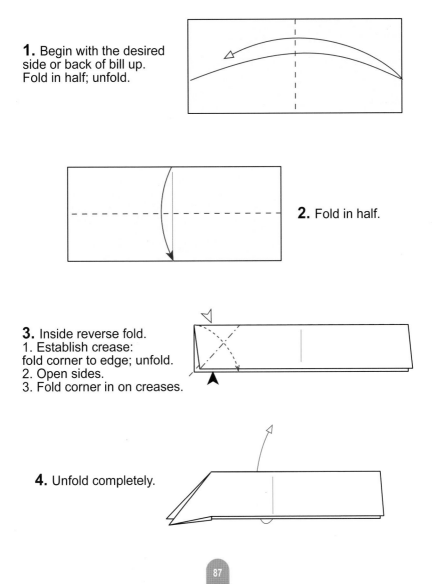

1. Begin with the desired side or back of bill up. Fold in half; unfold.

2. Fold in half.

3. Inside reverse fold.
1. Establish crease: fold corner to edge; unfold.
2. Open sides.
3. Fold corner in on creases.

4. Unfold completely.

5.
A. Fold; unfold each
edge to center line.
Crease as shown.
B. Fold edge to crease.

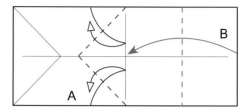

6.
A. Fold; unfold each
edge to crease.
B. Mtn. fold edge behind
to crease. Unfold side.

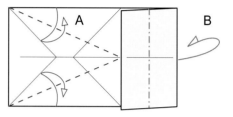

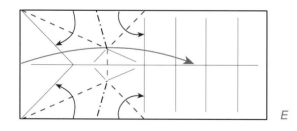

7.
1. Refold edges in on creases. Define intersection pts. of creases.
2. Fold edge down. Align center lines.
3. Flatten to set mtn. folds.

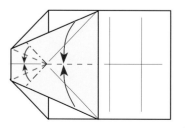

8. Fold sides together
down to base. Set folds.

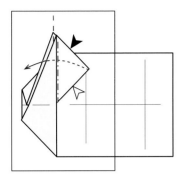

9. Inside reverse fold.
1. Open sides.
2. Fold edge in & through on creases.

10. Inside reverse fold.
1. Open sides.
2. Fold edges in to edges.

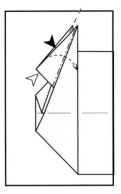

11.
Start at pt. Fold edge to edge.
Continue to fold outer layer over.

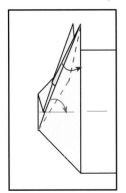

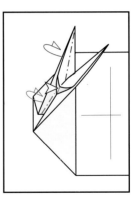

12. Symmetrically flatten triangular overlap. Mtn fold edges behind.

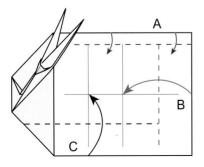

13.
A. Fold edge in on width of bill's back border.
B. Fold edge to crease.
C. Fold edge to crease.

14.
A. Fold edge pass center to overlap bill's border. Slip corner between indicated layers.
B. Fold straps up.

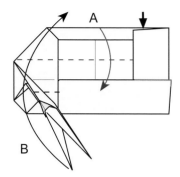

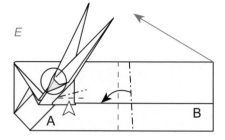

15.
A. Crimp base: Pinch strap. Push downward as you push in on fold line.
B. Pleat fold: Lift side on crease. Establish mtn. fold then fold new edge over on crease.

16.
A. Mtn. fold corner behind.
B. Pinch base. Stretch straps out to sides.

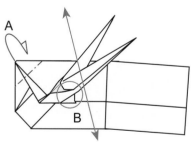

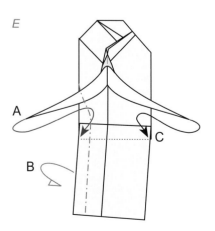

Model is rotated.

17.
A. Tuck tip of left strap in corner of pleat. Hold.
B. Mtn. fold edge behind.
(See Step 19 for view of result.)
C. Tuck tip of right strap in corner of pleat. Hold.

18.

A. Lift edge to fold corner of pleat up.
B. Mtn. fold corners behind.

Turn model over.

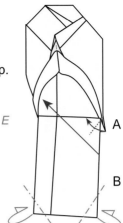

E

A

B

19. Fold corner with end of strap in under layer as seen in magnified result.

Turn model over.

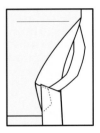

Proceed to next
page to fold
The Other Slipper.

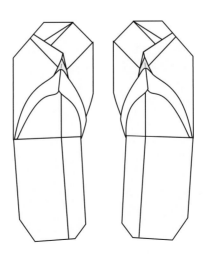

The Other Slipper

The *Slipper's* instructions have been modified to help you fold *The Other Slipper.* Begin with the bill either identically positioned or reflect the design or words as seen in the example.

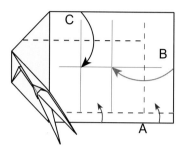

Proceed through steps 1 to 12 of the *Slipper.*

13.
A. Fold edge in on width of bill's back border.
B. Fold edge to crease.
C. Fold edge to crease.

14.
A. Fold edge past center to overlap bill's border. Slip corner between indicated layers.
B. Fold straps up.

15.
A. Crimp base: Pinch strap. Push downward as you push in on fold line.
B. Pleat fold: Lift side on crease. Establish mtn. fold then fold new edge over on crease.

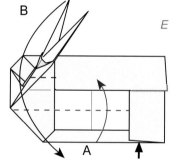

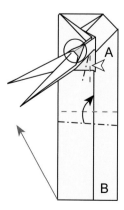

Model is rotated.

16.
A. Mtn. fold corner behind. Match fold of right slipper.
B. Pinch base. Stretch straps out to sides.

E

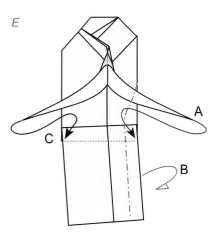

17.
A. Tuck tip of left strap in corner of pleat. Hold.
B. Mtn. fold edge behind. Match fold of right slipper. (See Step 19 for view of result.)
C. Tuck tip of right strap in corner of pleat. Hold.

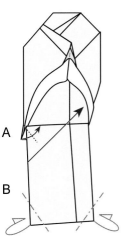

18.
A. Lift edge to fold corner of pleat up.
B. Mtn. fold corners behind. Match folds of right slipper.

Turn model over.

19. Fold corner with end of strap in under layer.

Turn model over.

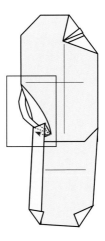

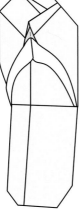

Maui Rose (Loke)

Maui Rose

Use the back of a one dollar bill or any larger denomination bill with the old design. You will need tape and a pair of tweezer to form and shape your rose. Paper substitutions: the *Maui Rose* displays one side of the paper.

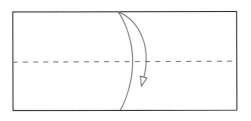

1. Begin with the desired side or back of bill down. Fold in half; unfold.

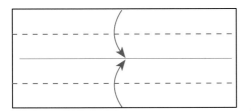

2. Fold edges to center.

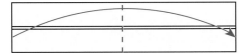

3. Fold in half.

4. Inside reverse fold each side.
1. Establish creases:
fold corner to center; unfold.
2. Open sides.
3. Fold corner in on creases.

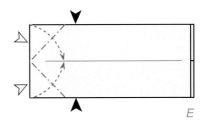

E

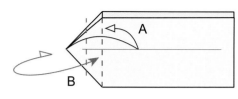

5.
A. Fold pt over; unfold.
B. Pre-crease:
1. Fold tip to crease.
2. Mtn. fold tip behind on same crease.
(Note: Crease extra well.)

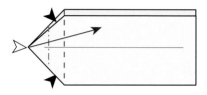

6. Flatten tip on creases:
1. Lift section perpendicular.
2. Keeping edges aligned, stretch open sides & center section on creases. (See 6a.)

6a.

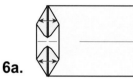

7. Mtn. fold sides open.

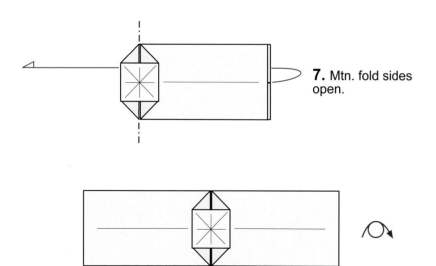

8. Turn model over.

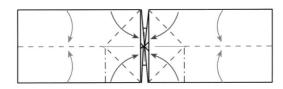

9. Rabbit ear fold each side.
1. Establish creases: fold; unfold each edge to center.
2. Refold edges up on creases as you fold sides together.
3. Mtn. fold is set by folding new flap down.

10. Fold flap over.

11. Fold edge to edge.

12.
A. Lift flap to overlap top layers.
B. Fold flap over.

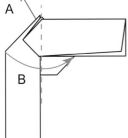

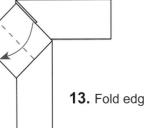

13. Fold edge to edge.

14. Squash fold flap.
1. Establish creases:
fold edge to crease; unfold.
2. Lift flap perpendicular.
3. Open layers.
4. Flatten on creases.

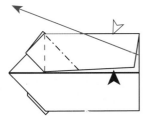

E

15.
Fold flap up.

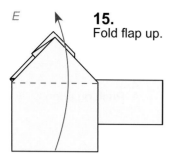

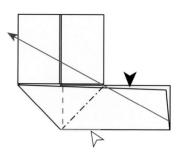

16. Establish fold: Fold flap to left.
Repeat steps 14 (shown) & 15
on flap.

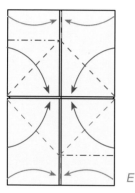

17. Rabbit ear fold each side.
1. Establish creases:
fold; unfold each edge to center.
2. Refold edges up on creases as you fold
sides together.
3. Mtn. fold is set by folding new flap down.

E

18. Fold flap down.

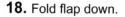
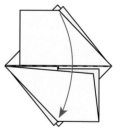

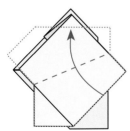

19. Fold edge up.

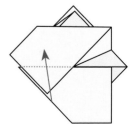

20. Lift pt. beneath to
overlap layer. Rotate
model 180 degrees to
repeat steps 18 & 19.

21. Overlap layers as shown.
Tape sides together.
Turn model over.

22.
A. Push on edge to
fold pt. to pt.
B. Round edge up.

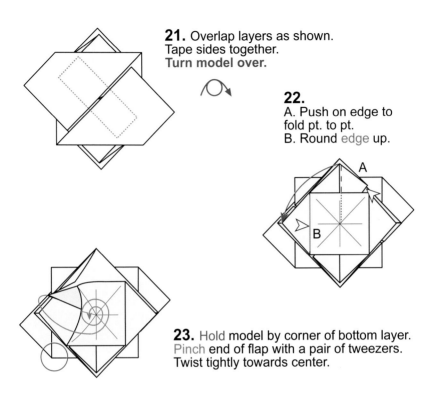

23. Hold model by corner of bottom layer.
Pinch end of flap with a pair of tweezers.
Twist tightly towards center.

24.
A. Mtn. fold edge behind.
With a pair of tweezers:
B. Pinch straight edges & twist
to pleat.
C. Curl all petals.

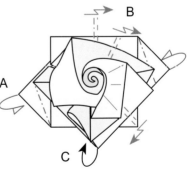

Simple Envelope

Simple Envelope

This simple envelope displays one side of the paper. A 6-inch square paper will produce an envelope 3 inches x 3.5 inches.

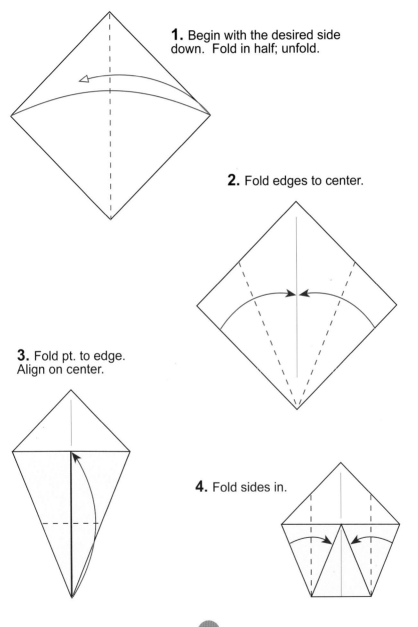

1. Begin with the desired side down. Fold in half; unfold.

2. Fold edges to center.

3. Fold pt. to edge. Align on center.

4. Fold sides in.

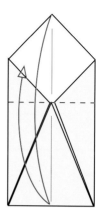

5. Fold down on V pt. Unfold.

6. Fold corner to center.

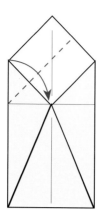

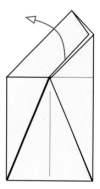

7. Unfold flap. Repeat steps 6 & 7 on right.

8. Fold pt. down to intersection of creases.

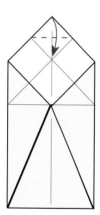

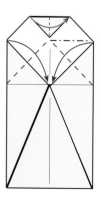

Place folded bill or coins in envelope.

9. Rabbit ear fold.
1. Refold edges up on creases as you fold sides together.
2. Mtn. fold is set by folding new flap down.

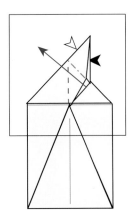

10. Squash fold each flap.
1. Establish fold. Lift flap perpendicular.
2. Open layers.
3. Flatten symmetrically.

11. Fold edges to center; unfold.

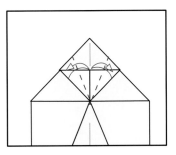

12. Insert pt. into pocket as you fold flap down. Pt. is folded over as flap is folded down completely. Flatten to set.

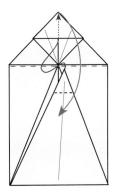

13. Refold flaps around center flap. Flatten to set.

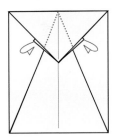

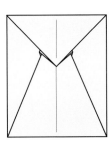

Money Wrap

Money Wrap

This model displays one side of the paper. A 6-inch square paper will produce an envelope 2.75 inches x 3.75 inches.

1. Begin with the desired side down. Fold in half; unfold. Repeat.

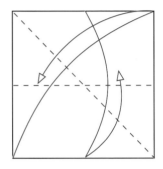

2.
A. Fold edges to center. Crease as shown. Unfold.
B. Fold edge to crease. Crease as shown. Unfold.

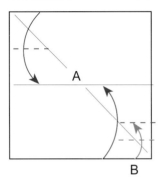

3. Fold in half.

Model is rotated.

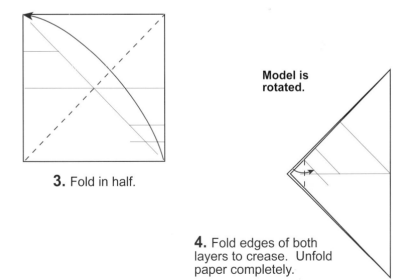

4. Fold edges of both layers to crease. Unfold paper completely.

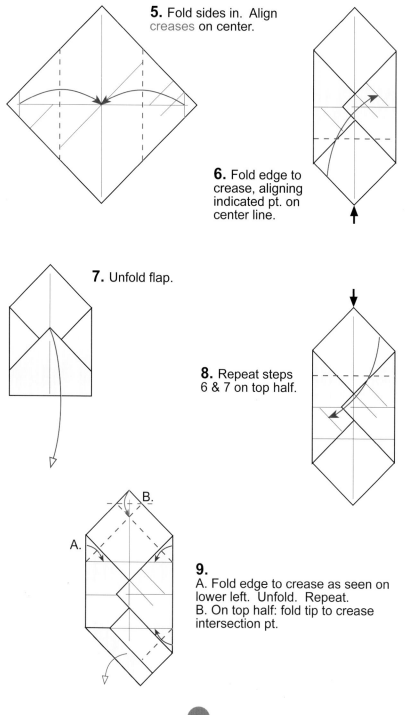

5. Fold sides in. Align creases on center.

6. Fold edge to crease, aligning indicated pt. on center line.

7. Unfold flap.

8. Repeat steps 6 & 7 on top half.

A.

B.

9.
A. Fold edge to crease as seen on lower left. Unfold. Repeat.
B. On top half: fold tip to crease intersection pt.

(Note: Place folded bill under center flaps of envelope.)

10. Rabbit ear fold each end.
1. Refold edges up on creases as you fold sides of tip together.
2. Mtn. fold is set by folding new flap down.

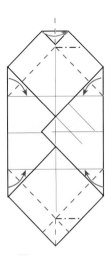

11. Squash fold each flap.
1. Establish fold. Lift flap perpendicular.
2. Open layers.
3. Flatten symmetrically.

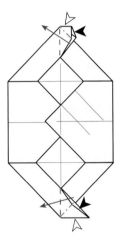

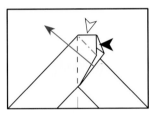

Magnified Top Half

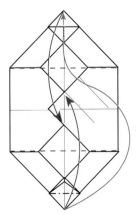

12. Insert tip of lower flap into pocket of top flap as you refold both flaps to center. Tip of lower flap is folded over as top flap is folded down completely .

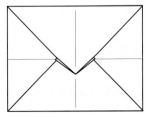

Flower Envelope

Flower Envelope

The *Flower Envelope* displays both sides of the paper. Select paper with contrasting side. A 7-inch square paper will produce an envelope 1.75 inches x 3.5 inches.

1. Begin with side/color of flower down. Fold in half; unfold. Repeat.

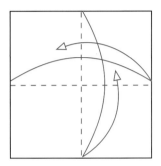

A

B

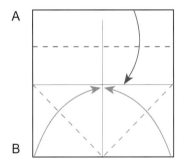

2.
A. Fold edge to center line.
B. Fold corner pts. to center.

A

B

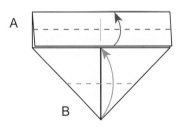

3.
A. Fold edge to edge.
B. Fold pt. up.

4. Mtn. fold edges behind to center.

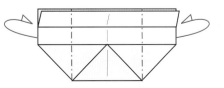

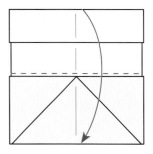

5. Fold in half.

6. Fold corner up. Push on edge to flatten section. (See 6a.) Repeat on right.

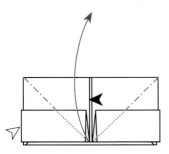

6a.

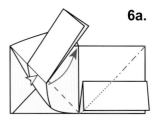

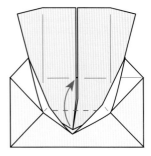

7. Open **top** layer on both sides.

8. Separate layers. Fold pt. up.

9. Fold creases to center.

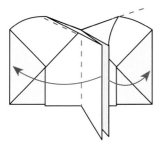

10. Fold edge to edge on each sides.

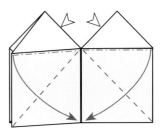

11. On both sides:
Fold corner pt. to corner pt.
Flatten section.

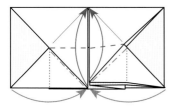

12. On both sides:
Fold pt. up. Fold corner
pt. to center.

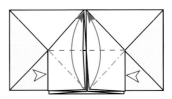

13. On both sides:
Fold pt. up. Flatten
section symmetrically.

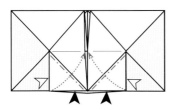

14. Inside reverse fold flaps.
1. Open layers.
2. Fold corner pt. in & up to center.

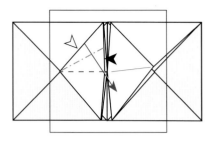

15. Squash fold middle flap.
1. Lift flap perpendicular.
2. Open layers.
3. Flatten section symmetrically.

16. Petal fold.
1. Establish creases: fold edges to center. (See 16a.) Unfold.
2. Fold pt. up between crease pts.
3. Fold edges in on creases. Gently stretch to align edges on center.

Repeat steps 15 & 16 on right.

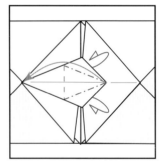

16a.

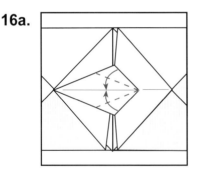

17. Squash fold all 4 flaps.
1. Establish fold:
fold flap in half; unfold.
Lift end section perpendicular.
2. Open layers. (See Note.)
3. Flatten symmetrically.

*(Note: Open layers as shown
with single layer bordering center.)*

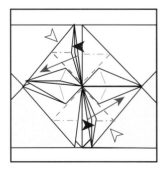

Optional: *lift section to glue in place. Repeat.*

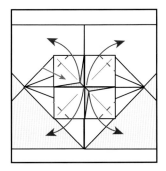

18. Fold flap open. Curling sides up.

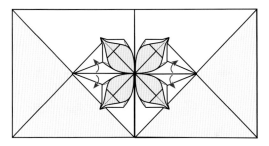

(Note: Stop here if a four petal envelope is desired.)

19. Open middle petals. Pinch sides of each petal together near tip to shorten, matching length of side petals. Shape all petals.

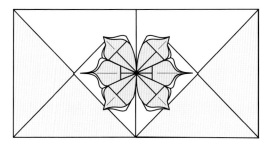

Lucky Frog Envelope

Lucky Frog Envelope

The *Lucky Frog Envelope* displays both sides of the paper. Select paper with contrasting sides. A 7-inch square paper will produce an envelope 2.5 inches x 3.5 inches.

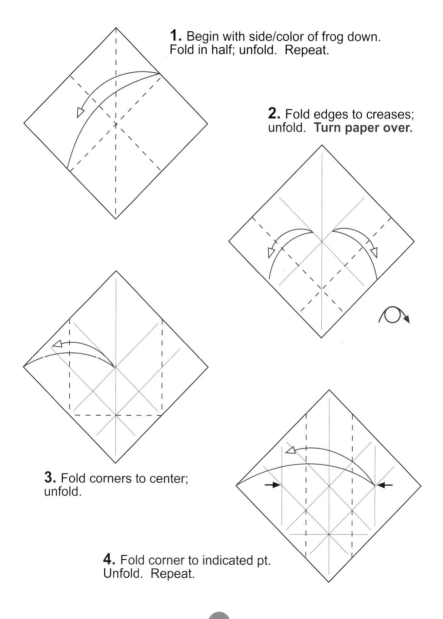

1. Begin with side/color of frog down. Fold in half; unfold. Repeat.

2. Fold edges to creases; unfold. **Turn paper over.**

3. Fold corners to center; unfold.

4. Fold corner to indicated pt. Unfold. Repeat.

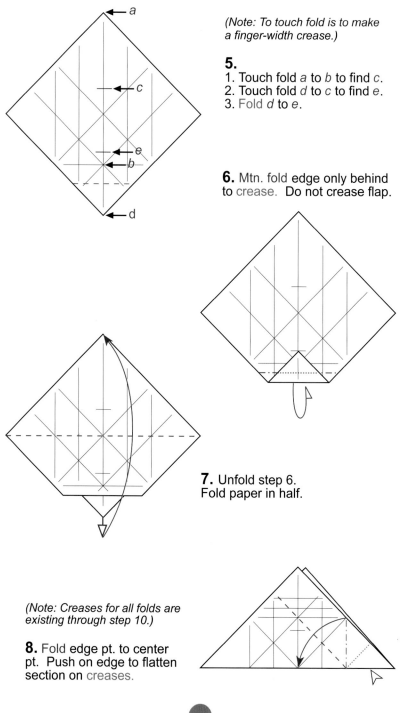

(Note: To touch fold is to make a finger-width crease.)

5.
1. Touch fold *a* to *b* to find *c*.
2. Touch fold *d* to *c* to find *e*.
3. Fold *d* to *e*.

6. Mtn. fold edge only behind to crease. Do not crease flap.

7. Unfold step 6. Fold paper in half.

(Note: Creases for all folds are existing through step 10.)

8. Fold edge pt. to center pt. Push on edge to flatten section on creases.

9. Fold pt. of top layer over. Push on edges to flatten sections on creases.

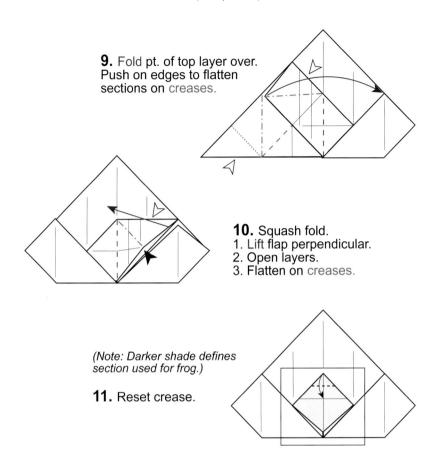

10. Squash fold.
1. Lift flap perpendicular.
2. Open layers.
3. Flatten on creases.

(Note: Darker shade defines section used for frog.)

11. Reset crease.

12. *(Note: Creases for all folds are existing except mtn. folds.)*
1. Lift flap up on crease 1.
2. Pinch sides together to reestablish mtn. fold to pt. shown.
3. Fold sides in to center on creases. (See 12a.)
New mtn. folds are made in the process. Set all folds.

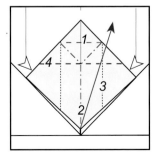

12a.

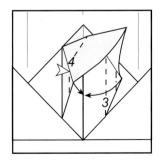

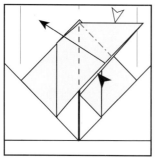

13. Squash fold.
1. Lift flap perpendicular.
2. Open layers.
3. Flatten section symmetrically.

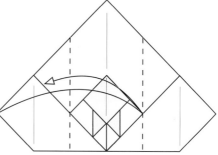

14. Fold; unfold each side in on crease.

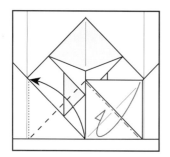

15. Pre-crease each side:
1. Fold edge to pt. shown.
2. Mtn. fold flap under on same crease. Unfold.

16. On each side:
1. Separate layer. ➤
Re-establish mtn. fold.
2. Refold flap up on crease.
3. New fold is made in process.

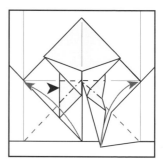

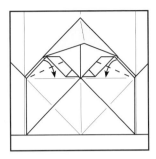

17. Fold edge to crease on both sides.

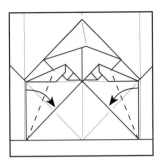

18. Fold each edge to edge.

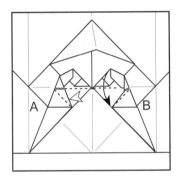

19. On both sides:
A. Push edge over as you...
B. Fold corner down on crease. (*Note: New edges.*)

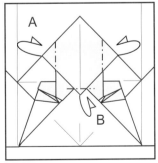

20.
A. Fold corners under edges beneath.
B. Mtn. fold pt. under.

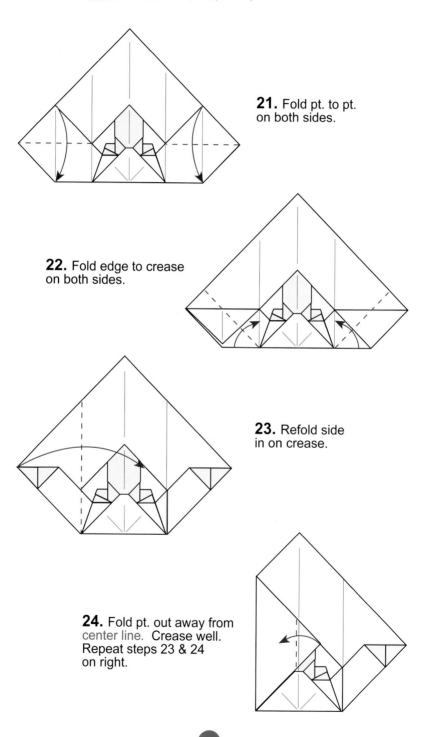

21. Fold pt. to pt. on both sides.

22. Fold edge to crease on both sides.

23. Refold side in on crease.

24. Fold pt. out away from center line. Crease well. Repeat steps 23 & 24 on right.

25. On both sides:
A. Unfold flap as seen on right.
B. Refold edge under body & leg.

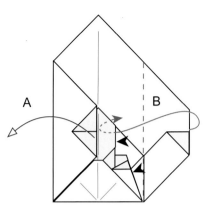

A   B

26. Fold flap into frog's mouth.

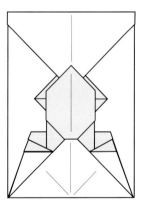

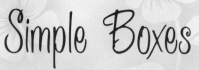

Simple Boxes

 Simple Boxes

You will need two square sheets of paper to create a box with a lid. Ideally, one sheet should be 1/4-inch square smaller. Trim adjacent sides as shown. Fold the bottom of the box from the smaller sheet and the lid from the larger sheet.

Trim 1/4 inch off adjacent sides.

Use a square box folded from a 6-inch square sheet of paper to present *The Luckiest Frog, Coconut Frond Fish,* or a combination of *Roses, Stars,* and *Plumerias.* The *Turtle* and *Flower* require a square box folded from a 7-inch square sheet. The *Pineapple* and *Slipper* (one side only) will fit in a rectangular box made from a 6-inch square sheet.

Square Box *(Note: Two lid designs are offered.)*

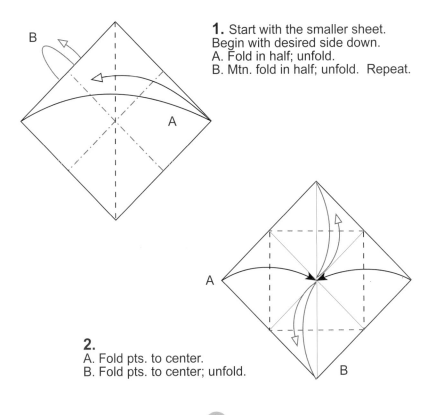

B

A

1. Start with the smaller sheet. Begin with desired side down.
A. Fold in half; unfold.
B. Mtn. fold in half; unfold. Repeat.

A

B

2.
A. Fold pts. to center.
B. Fold pts. to center; unfold.

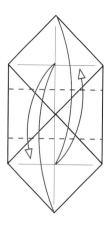

3. Fold; unfold each pt. to crease.

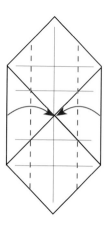

4. Fold edges to center.

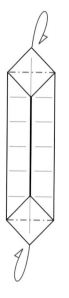

5. Mtn. fold each pt. behind to crease.

6.
A. Lift sides perpendicular.
B. Fold ends up on creases.

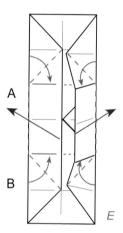

A

B

E

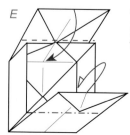

E

7. Fold sides in on creases. Unfold flap to line bottom of

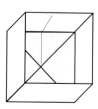

For a lid of similar dimensions, repeat, using the larger sheet. For a shallow lid, see following page.

To fold a shallow lid, use the larger sheet. Follow previous instructions from Step 1 through Step 4.

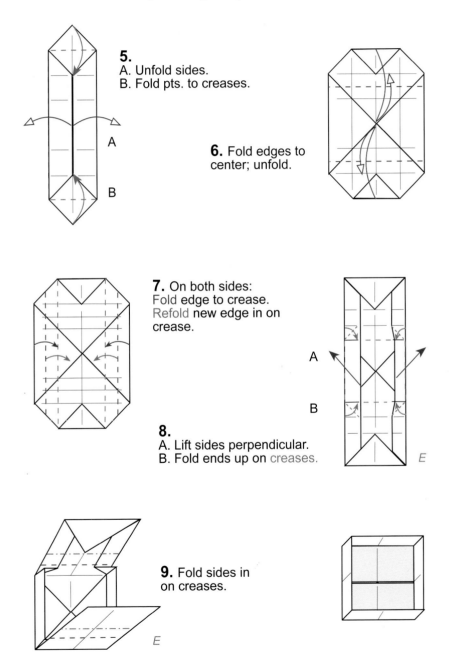

5.
A. Unfold sides.
B. Fold pts. to creases.

6. Fold edges to center; unfold.

7. On both sides: Fold edge to crease. Refold new edge in on crease.

8.
A. Lift sides perpendicular.
B. Fold ends up on creases.

9. Fold sides in on creases.

Rectangular Box

1. Begin with desired side down. Fold in half; unfold. Repeat.

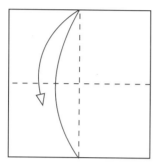

2. Fold edges to center.

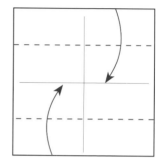

E

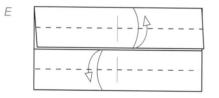

3. Fold edges to center; unfold.

4. Fold edges to center; unfold.

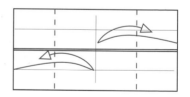

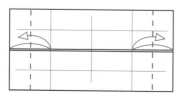

5. Fold edges to creases; unfold. **Turn model over.**

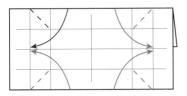

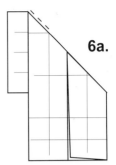

6a.

6. Align edge on crease.
Fold only as shown. (See 6a.)
Unfold. Repeat.

Turn model over.

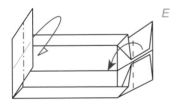

7. Fold sides up on center rectangle, folding crease pts. to center.

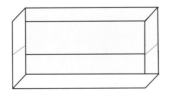

E

8. Fold ends down.
Optional: glue to hold.

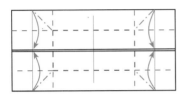

Repeat all steps on second
sheet to create other half of box.